Get More Clients Online

How to Leverage Your Business and Generate New Clients

Sarit Lotem

Get More Clients Online

Printed by:
90-Minute Books
302 Martinique Drive
Winter Haven, FL 33884
www.90minutebooks.com

Copyright © 2016, Sarit Lotem

Published in the United States of America

160218-00345

ISBN-10: 1535508132
ISBN-13: 9781535508131

No parts of this publication may be reproduced without correct attribution to the author of this book.

For more information on 90-Minute Books including finding out how you can publish your own lead generating book, visit www.90minutebooks.com or call (863) 318-0464

Here's What's Inside...

A Note From Me 1

Part 1: How the Right Website Can Help
Position You as an Expert in Your Field 5

Part 2: Identifying Your Ideal Client 11

Part 3: Your Business's Domain Name 16

Part 4: Home Page Essentials.......................21

Part 5: Social Media......................................34

Part 6: How to Reach
More Clients Online 38

Part 7: Common Website Mistakes
and How to Avoid Them 43

Important Links 53

How to Leverage Your Business
and Generate New Clients Online 55

A Note From Me

Are you frustrated with the results generated by your website? I constantly hear this complaint from business owners around the country. Often, their web designers were unresponsive, and their expertise was limited to just creating nice web pages. What they promised to deliver never got delivered, so the website sits in Park, not doing what it was designed to do: generate new clients and business.

I've been creating websites and marketing businesses online for the last ten years. I have worked with hundreds of small and medium-sized business owners from mom-and-pop shops, individual professionals and solo entrepreneurs to manufacturers and large associations.

My work during all those years provided me with powerful insight to what works and what doesn't when it comes to attracting new customers. I learned the best methods of generating business online as well as how to convert visitors from casual web surfers to repeat customers.

Like those designers I mentioned before, when I started my business, I just knew how to design. The websites I designed were beautiful, and my clients were happy. However, I noticed that in some cases, these new sites were not generating more business for their owners. That was also the result I experienced with my own website. I spent years studying and perfecting sites in a deliberate effort to find the formula that would allow websites to become client-generating machines.

I'm proud to say I found it!

Implementing my acquired knowledge on my own business website helped me increase my revenue tenfold. Yes, you are reading it right: 10 times more! The amount of clients that I generate today is far beyond what I thought was possible.

Even more important, my clients are experiencing similar results and are getting more clients than ever before. They often tell me that they religiously apply my techniques and practices when they see how well they work.

Why am I telling you this? Because I believe in sharing knowledge between communities, and that with the right support everyone can achieve success and financial stability.

I believe that when you achieve success, you give hope and touch the lives of your family, your community, your town/city and eventually the whole world.

My goal in writing this book is to share my "How's" with you: how online business works, how to generate traffic to your website, how to choose the best domain name for your business, etc.

I cover all this and more right here in an easy, non-technical way so you can get the same results I get for my clients. Even if you decide to hire a professional to do the work, you will still have the valuable knowledge to make the right decisions and learn how to leverage your business in your favor.

One more thing: in the spirit of growing, business-wise and spirit-wise, I buy many books. I have stacks of them by my bedside. However, it is rare that I finish any of them. I usually start with a lot of enthusiasm and tend to lose it after 40-50 pages.

Therefore, I've decided to make my book short and to the point with a lot of actionable tips that you can implement immediately.

To your success,

Sarit

About the structure of the book:

This book is divided into seven parts. Each part can stand alone, but together they are powerful as they will help you understand what it takes to create a successful online business.

In part one, I'll describe the benefits of a good website and how the right website can help position you and your business as an expert in your field.

In part two, I'll go over some ideas on how to understand what your ideal clients really want and how to use that in your website.

In part three, I'll show you how to pick the best domain name for your business.

In part four, I'll cover the importance of creating a powerful home page and how to achieve it.

In part five, I'll go over how to use social media effectively.

In part six, I'll teach you how to reach more clients online.

In part seven, I'll go over the common mistakes people make when creating a website and share advice on how to avoid them.

Part 1: How the Right Website Can Help Position You as an Expert in Your Field

You've probably already heard that people do business with people they know, like and trust. A movie with a highly decorated director will attract more viewers than a three-star movie; a restaurant with a celebrated chef will fill up faster than a neighborhood diner. We like to be associated with experts and brilliant people because it's exciting and it makes us feel good about ourselves.

The same concept holds true for your business. Your website is the perfect place to introduce yourself to new visitors and prospects, it's where you can share your offers and services, position yourself as an expert, and inform them that you are the go-to person in your field while assuring them that they came to the right place.

People are spending twice as much time online now than they did 10 years ago.

In total, the average adult spends more than 20 hours online a week (apart from work or study). According to Ofcom's Media Use and Attitudes Report in 2015, this has increased by five times since 2005, when the figure was just 30 minutes.

This number will keep growing with the increasing use of tablets and smartphones.

So with all the online traffic out there, how do you leverage your website to position you as an expert and the go-to person in your field?

There are a number of ways. Some are easy to implement and some will require more dedication and effort. What's important to know is that in this day and age, with so many websites and experts out there, positioning yourself the right way can mean the difference between a new client and a "dead" online business.

Here are some of the best ways to gain online authority in your field:

Be knowledgeable: Always be aware of your clients' needs and trends. Always be one step ahead of your competitors! If you're in the nutrition and health industry, you should be reading two to four books per month on the latest trends in the field, reading magazines every week and taking in everything else that is relevant to the industry. Take that knowledge and use it on your website. You can share links to articles you read and liked, you can test theories and write about them, you can answer questions or you can simplify it for your readers.

Be known: You've worked with clients, you know people. Share that. Let your potential customers know that you are not new to the business and that you have worked with real clients and are proud of sharing their names. If one of your clients is somebody who is well known, impress your customers by sharing that information. Even if your clients are unknown, they are just as important. Share a story about them; share their names (if they agree to it), and share the issues they faced and how you helped them. This will make your business much more real and relatable.

> Important: a good practice, which should be common sense, is to ask your clients for their approval before you share their information.

Be open: Share testimonials and reviews from previous clients. It is an extremely powerful tool to encourage a customer's trust. I highly recommend adding a picture of them. This will make it even more real. Not only will you showcase that clients were pleased with your work, their experiences may resonate well with customers that experience similar issues. THIS IS A MUST-HAVE!

Another powerful method is to share video and audio testimonials.

Be trustworthy: You want YOUR customers and clients to trust you and come to you for the latest information, guidance and expertise, and your website is the perfect platform for this.

Use your website to inspire and motivate your prospects by sharing great content and tips.

Use visual aids to position yourself as an expert on your website if:

-You won an award

-You were featured in an event or summit

-You are certified in your field

-Your article was published in a magazine

-You receive good reviews

Highlight as much of the above as possible on your website.

As competition is fierce and the market is most likely saturated with similar businesses, your website is not the place to be introverted or shy; it's the place to highlight your gifts and accolades and share them with your prospects and the world.

Your competitors are doing it, so why shouldn't you?

Don't give your visitors a reason to check your competitors' sites. Give them all the information they need to trust and like you so they can feel comfortable enough to take the next step.

On my website, I created an image with many of the logos of the organizations, centers, schools and other businesses that I partner with. I position this image above the fold (the top section of my home page) so when my visitors come to my website, they can't miss it. Since I could not use all my partners' logos (there's not enough room for all of them), I made sure to use the logos that would give me the most recognition.

Be authentic: Don't be afraid to be yourself and to share the real you with your prospects. Whenever you can, share your story and how you came to be the business owner that you are, along with whom you helped along the way and what you learned. People like to connect with real people, not machines. This is why current advertisements emphasize the human touch.

A good idea is to share why you're in this business as well as how you plan to achieve your goals.

Be unique: Share what makes you and your business special. Address this in a way that shows how you are different/better than your competitors. Emphasize your strengths and what clients will get if they work with you. Many people are reluctant to share such information, feeling that they are bragging. Being unique and doing things in a certain special way is the beauty of your business. It is the reason people want to do business with you. If you want to have success online, you need to be comfortable sharing your special traits with the whole world.

Some ideas include:

-You care more than the competitors

-You only work with a specific audience (kids from ages 3-6, German shepherd dogs, etc.)

-You specialize in a specific machine

-You only sell one brand (e.g. phone cases exclusively for iPhones)

-You offer a full service

-You answer calls personally

People who feel confused and don't trust you won't buy from you. It's that simple.

Your market is probably saturated with service-providers and merchants just like you. When prospects first visit your website, your goal is to make them instantly feel that you are trustworthy and that you have all the answers to their problems. All they need to do is reach out.

Your story does not have to be sad for your clients to relate to it. It just needs to explain how you ended up doing what you do.

Include what affected you and why you are passionate about your business. People want to do business with real people, not with machines.

A powerful and very effective way to achieve this is by adding a short video on your site. Welcome your site's visitors, introduce yourself and your services.

Here's an example for a script:

"Welcome to ___. My name is ___ and I'm the owner/founder of ___.

I'm passionate about helping people ___ so they can ___.

My services include ___.

I would love to speak with you to see if I can help."

This will give your prospect a glimpse into who you really are and how you can help them, but more importantly, it gives them a chance to connect with an authentic person and not just a web page.

Now that you understand how your website can help position you as the go-to person in your field, let's explore what else you can do to leverage your business and generate new clients online.

Part 2: Identifying Your Ideal Client

During the years, I was fortunate to work with hundreds of business owners, many of whom make the same common mistakes when it comes to building their business website - they don't think about their customers. Instead, they concentrate on things they like themselves. The fact is that it's not their fault. Nobody explained to them how important it is to address their prospects and target market in their website. They are not web design experts or online marketers so there is no reason for them to know this.

The sad reality is that they spend their time, money and energy, and when prospects visit their websites, they don't feel that the business owners understand them and could actually assist them.

If you want to succeed online, then you need to take the time to research and really understand your ideal client. The more you understand them, the more you can help them. Once you really nail this part, you will be able to use this knowledge on your website to help visitors feel that you are talking directly to them and that you really understand their needs.

So, who are your ideal clients?

In order to answer this essential question, I want you to think about your top clients. Make a list of the clients that you've enjoyed working with and that generated the most income for you and see if you can fill out the table on the next page.

	Client 1	Client 2	Client 3
Age, social status, education, career, etc.			
Gender			
Location (Country, city, etc.)			
Problems they have that relate to your line of work (specific to your offerings)			
Financial status			
Possible phrases they would use to ask someone about their problem (Google it)			
Steps already taken in order to solve their problems and results of those steps			
Favorite online spots: social media channels, blogs, etc.			
Favorite offline spots: stores, coffee shops, etc.			

Remember, your goal in this step is to really get familiar with your prospects' hopes and needs to understand what they love and enjoy, what annoys them and what's not working in their lives right now. Getting the answers to those questions and finding the common denominators will help you focus your website's message and your online presence in order to satisfy these ideal clients.

*This question is so important, and the answer is incredibly valuable. It will give you insight into what worked for them in the past and what didn't, what they liked and how serious they are in terms of getting results. It will also tell you about their journey up to this point.

Here are some examples:

Example #1

Let's say that you are a chiropractor. From the research you've done, you know that your ideal clients are males who suffer from back and neck pain. You also know that many of them work in a store, which means they stand most of the day.

How do you use this knowledge on your business's website? You can write an article about the five best ways to ease back and neck pain for people who stand most of the day. Another option might include, "4 Easy Exercises to Ease Back Pain Caused by Standing". Showcase your training certifications on your site. Share testimonials from people who work in stores and/or stand all day and have suffered from back and neck pain and now are pain-free, thanks to you.

Example #2

Let's say that you are a nutritionist and after you've done your research, you know that your ideal client is a woman who takes the bus to work every day and has no time to go to the gym. She feels tired and lacks energy.

How do you use this knowledge to establish your business and help your prospects?

Create and share some YouTube videos on your website about the best morning shakes that keep you active all day long. Share a recipe for an energy bar that your ideal client can make by herself in five minutes and can eat on the bus ride or keep in her office drawer for when she needs a boost.

You see, without being sleazy or pushy, you are communicating that you are the go-to person in your field and that you can help customers with their burning questions and problems.

The right look: Different fonts, color schemes, social media platforms, jargon, images and layouts can also help convince your prospects that you know and understand them.

For example: cool and modern fonts will resonate with a younger audience, while fonts like Times New Roman will resonate with the more serious and adult audience.

Light green and white are the perfect colors for clinics, caretakers, yoga studios, etc. People associate them with relaxation (this is why hospital walls are painted light green).

If you know that your ideal clients spends time on Facebook, then have a Facebook plugin on your website that updates your Facebook page whenever you have a new post. However, business owners often think they need to be everywhere on social media. They don't. They only need to be active on the platforms that their ideal clients are on. If their ideal client is not on Twitter, they don't need to spend time on Twitter.

Again, you want to make your prospects feel welcome and understood when they visit your website. It's all about them and their expectations, feelings and needs.

Part 3: Your Business's Domain Name

People ask me all the time, "Is my domain name really that important?" My answer is always an absolute, "Yes."

Think about it - when you meet new people and tell them about your business, and they really like it and want your help, the next thing they will probably ask is, "What's your website?" or "Where can I find you online?"

If your domain name is complicated or not easy to remember, they will never go home and find you. Even if they try, they will probably never find your business online.

However, if your domain is easy to remember, chances are that they will contact you days or even weeks after you first meet.

In general, there are two types of domains - brandable and discoverable domains.

1. **"Brandable" domain name:** Brandable domain names are domain names that can be used for a wide variety of websites. Think of names like Google, Nike and Lululemon. The names don't convey the business's purpose so they can be used for pretty much anything. Brandable domains are easy to remember. The downside is that, at least in the beginning, only people who are familiar with your brand can find your domain and website. Others that are not familiar with the brand will likely never see the site or buy from it.

Brandable names are distinctive and easy to remember, but you will need to have a good and solid marketing plan to promote and introduce your brand to your target market if you choose this one.

2. **"Discoverable" domain name:** Discoverable domain names can be found by anyone, even if they are not familiar with you or your business as they can simply search for similar services on search engines. Discoverable names are descriptive. They use words or phrases that describe your business or niche. For example: Hotels.com, OverStock.com, BusinessCoach.com or WebsiteDesign.com. Most small and medium-sized businesses start with a discoverable domain name as they're easier to find online.

If you choose to go with a discoverable domain name for your business, one of the best ways to find the perfect domain name is to ask your previous and current clients what words or phrases they searched for online to find a business like yours.

Your next step is to leverage Google to find more keywords for your domain name. Go to Google and start typing a simple keyword. Do not click "search" yet. Just type a word. For example, if you are in the soy soap business, type the phrase "soy soap" in the search box. Google will automatically show you a drop-down of some suggestions to finish your search. Those extra words are high-ranked search terms that people are looking for on Google right now. Add those keywords to your list.

There are several more tools out there to generate even more keywords like Google Keyword Planner and Wordtracker.

Now that you have your keywords, your next step is to pair and combine them until you come up with a good combination that makes sense for your business.

But before you start this pairing process, let's go over some important guidelines.

The following seven tips can be used as guidelines when picking a domain name:

1. Include a primary keyword – If you are an electrician, including words like "electric" or "electrician" could be the first step in getting found online.

2. Include a geographic marker – If you have a local business, including your city/county/state can help people find you in local searches.

3. Make it easy to type – Avoid using slang and cute misspellings like "4" instead of "for", or "u" instead of "you."

4. Keep it short – Shorter domain names are easier to remember and share.

5. Avoid hyphens and dashes – They are confusing and make it more difficult for people to remember.

6. Choose a memorable suffix – If possible, choose a .com suffix. People automatically assume your suffix will be .com.

If you live outside the USA, and you only service the local market, in addition to the .com suffix, you might also want to buy the local suffix. For example: LotemDesign.co.uk.

7. Register Common Misspellings – If your domain contains words that are commonly misspelled, consider registering those misspellings as well and redirecting them to your primary domain.

In short, you want your domain to be memorable, shareable and descriptive of what you do and where you do it. Keep this in mind and you should be able to find the perfect domain for your business.

> Important: If your preferred domain is not already in use, be quick; don't hesitate and purchase it right away. I can't tell you how many times my clients hesitated for just a couple of minutes, and by the time they went back to buy the domain, it was already gone.

When I first bought my domain name, I made all the classic mistakes: my domain did not contain the key words "website design" or "web design", which is the essence of my business and instead it contained my last name, "Lotem."

If we had just met and I mentioned my URL to you, you would never remember my name when you got home, let alone after a couple of days or weeks. However, as my website gained authority and influence during the years, it didn't make sense to start all over again with a new domain name.

My solution was to buy a new domain name that contains my keywords and redirects visitors to my old domain: www.lotemdesign.com.

Learn from my mistake; take your time and make sure to pick your perfect domain the first time around.

Important links

Domain name and hosting companies:

http://www.bluehost.com (my preferred company)

http://www.godaddy.com

To check your chosen domain availability and alternatives: www.leandomainsearch.com

Part 4: Home Page Essentials

Your home page is the most visited page on your website. It's most likely where the first interaction with your prospects will take place.

In fact, 80 percent of the traffic that comes to your website will come through your homepage.

Optimizing the layout of your homepage can increase the interaction with your prospects by 200-300 percent.

A successful homepage should be able to achieve three goals:

-Position you as an expert in your field

-Share ways to contact you

-Tell prospects how to take the next step with you

Quiz:

How long do new visitors spend on a website before they decide to stay and read more or to move on to your competitors' sites?

5 seconds

10 seconds

20 seconds

Correct Answer: a. 5 seconds.

You only have five seconds to position your business as the leader in your industry, to show prospects how to contact you and to tell them exactly what you want them to do.

Be strategic and think about your goals. Your homepage is prime real estate. The color scheme, layout, images, jargon, fonts and everything else should be there for a particular reason. So let's talk about your homepage and how to make it a client-magnet.

Home Page Must-Have 1: Ways to contact you by phone number and email.

Not long ago, I read an article that says that nearly 40 percent of websites do not have a phone number on their home page.

Don't you hate that?

If your prospect can't find your phone number in less than two seconds, you risk losing potential business. The same goes for your company's email address.

Business owners sometimes think that sharing their phone number and other contact information on the "Contact Us" page is enough. I'm here to tell you that it's not.

Why? It's because people are lazy, and they just don't like to look for things. Eliminate extra clicks and give your prospects all your contact information on the silver platter that is your home page.

Where should you place your phone number?

Your phone number can be in the header of your site, on the side bar or in the footer. It doesn't matter as long as it's visible. Also, think about prospects on mobile devices.

For prospects visiting your website on their cell phone or another device, it's easy to click on the phone number they see on your home page, and the device will make the call automatically. No need to copy the numbers or punch them one-by-one on your phone.

The same goes with your company's email address. People can click on it, and a window with your company's email address will open up for them to send an email to you.

Another excellent and easy way to have people contact you is by adding a quick form on your homepage (or anywhere on the website).

A name, email address and a message field are all that is needed. The reason for this quick form is that in general, people don't like to fill out long forms. It's annoying and they won't put down all of their information. However, if you just ask them for their name and email, they are more likely to fill it out. The psychology behind it is that when they submit this quick form, they are basically telling you, "Okay, I like what I see. I like what you have to offer. Please contact me and it's okay to pitch your services."

Important: This is not a sales pitch form; this is only a quick form with a simple message: "If you have a question, contact us." It's just a form for your prospects to quickly reach out to you.

Home Page Must-Have 2: Above-the-fold form or "The Profit Funnel."

A big mistake many small businesses make is the assumption that if they create a great product, people will come, and that's not the case. We have to be able to convert leads into clients. If you can't convert leads into clients, you really don't have a successful business. There are a lot of entrepreneurs out there who are doing all sorts of things to generate leads but are not doing anything to turn those leads into clients. If you can't convert leads into clients, then you don't really have an online business.

One of the best ways to transform your home page's visitors into clients is to create what I call "The Profit Funnel." This idea is relatively new and my clients and I receive great results from it.

Get your prospects to subscribe to your list (as opposed to sending you a quick message or subscribing to a blog post). From there, they will enter an automatic system that will allow them to get to know you better, trust you and of course, follow you. They will be willing to take the next step with you, whether it's to buy from you, hire your services or sign up for your training.

In order to get your visitors to subscribe to your list, offer them something in return. The key is to offer something that they really want and that can give them instant results. It could be a free session with you, a recipe for the best smoothie or a five-minute morning meditation video. How do you figure out which free gift you should offer?

For this, you will need to go to Part Two of the book – Identifying Your Ideal Client. What keeps them up at night? What problems are they facing right now that you can help them solve? Once you figure this out, you can package it in an easy-to-consume way.

Your gift should be a great motivator for prospects to fill out your form and get on your list.

Using a big sign-up form on the top of your website (above-the-fold) eliminates the noise from your site. No more dozens of links to click or confusing messages.

Here are the steps to follow:

#1 Your leads come in through your above-the-fold form with a free gift!

#2 They sign up and get your first newsletter.

#3 You educate and form a relationship with your prospects.

#4 You pitch your business and services.

Let's explore this further.

#1 Your leads come in through your above-the-fold form with a free gift!

In order for your prospects to take you up on your offer and to opt-in to your list, your free gift should be a product or an idea that is of high value to your clients.

For me, my customers are looking to generate more business and income online, so it makes sense to give them a checklist on how to build a home page that will get their prospects to take the next step with them.

How do you know what to give your prospects or know what they are looking for? One of my favorite ways (other than researching your ideal client) is to leverage Amazon. I look for books in my line of work that receive four to five-star ratings and have excellent reviews. I will then check the comment section and make a list of the most common questions and complaints that readers share.

Those questions are your prospects' burning problems and your freebie should cover the answers to them.

This is called "Instant Market Research", and by implementing this method, you will save many hours of searching and experimenting.

Your gift can be in different formats.

Some examples include:

-An mp3 or audio file

-A video series

-A checklist

-A book/e-book

-A webinar

-A product (cream, candle, etc.)

#2 They sign up and get your first newsletter.

For this, use a mail service such as Mailchimp, Aweber, Getresponse or ActiveCampaign.

Your first automated email should be short and to the point. Thank them for signing up, and if the gift is a PDF or another digital product, attach the link to it.

#3 You educate and form a relationship with your prospects.

The next two to four emails are for sharing more high quality, informative content that is strongly related to the gift.

It could be a case study, links to an article or a different idea to solve a problem that is related to your free gift.

How much information should you give? As much as you can. I don't believe in skimping here. I believe in value and giving without holding back.

The idea is to get your prospects to think, "If this is what I can get for free, I must work with him/her so I can get even more of these brilliant ideas!" Hence "The Profit Funnel".

Think about the music industry. Artists release their best songs as singles before they launch the full album.

Why not do the same with your business? Remember: this might be your prospect's first contact with you, so make sure it's really good.

Some ideas for easy free content to share:

-7-interview series solving a HUGE problem for your niche

-One of your smaller programs/products that you normally offer on sale

-A newsletter about getting access to your best business tips

#4 You pitch your business.

Now it's time to tell readers about your services and products and how you can assist them.

At this point, you've already established your knowledge and expertise, so the chances that readers will respond are extremely high.

> Important: make sure that the services you offer are in line with the free gift offer on your home page. There is no use in doing all this work and offering something that is not related. You will not find me offering free candles for my web design business…

Home Page Must-Have 3: Tell your prospects how to take the next step.

Business owners often assume that their visitors or prospects know what to do on their websites, but the fact is they do not, and they will not spend time guessing.

Be very specific in directing your site's visitors; otherwise they will just navigate away.

One of the best practices to achieve this is with a call-to-action, or CTA.

A CTA is a simple instruction or a lead that tells people exactly what you want them to do on your home page.

Some examples for effective CTA's:

-Call/contact me

-Click here to buy

-Fill out a form

-Register for a free training

-Click here to read more

-Download an MP3

A CTA can also lead your prospect through your website, like a road map or a story.

For example, you can share a teaser about you on your home page, and if prospects want to read a little bit more about you or the business, use a "Click here to read more about me" button and send them to an About page, and on the About page, when they get to know you better, you can say, "Are you ready to take the next step with me? Let's talk a little bit more." In this case, your CTA is "Call me."

There can be more than one CTA on your home page. On my home page, I have three different call-to-actions. The first one is a "Home Page Must-Haves" free checklist, which I position on the top banner.

The second CTA is a quick form on the bottom of my home page for visitors to contact me.

The third CTA is in the middle of the page where I showcase my three main services in three boxes. Each service box contains a different CTA. For my web design services box, the call-to-action is a button that says, "Jump-start your business." On my digital marketing service box, the call-to-action button says, "Grow your business," and the home page redesign service box says, "Upgrade your business."

Each package redirects my prospects to a designated page with more information and an explanation on how to take the next step.

> Important: The more time prospects spend on your website, the more they will like and trust you, and the higher the chances are that they will take the next step with you.

Home Page Must-Have 4: Images. Increase engagement on your website by using images, as the human brain is wired to respond to images faster than it will respond to textual content. In addition, images can help make memorable associations and elicit emotions. As a result, one image can be more powerful than the associated written words.

Type of images to use:

Products in action: There is nothing more effective than showing people using your products in action. If you can, create a little story behind the people in the picture. Let the visitor relate to your story and make them want to be a part of it.

Before and after: Use before and after photos - show how previous customers benefited from your products and why new customers should start using your products. Whether you are an interior designer or a landscaper, show the space before you performed your 'magic', and then after.

Gallery of work: Whether you are a photographer or graphic designer, inform your visitors by showcasing your work on your home page with a small gallery or portfolio. You can use cool effects like light box slideshows and GIF animations. Don't send your visitors to a designated page. They might not stay long enough to see your work.

Profile image: Let the visitors meet you and your stuff. Don't use corporate photos that look too formed and unnatural. Remember, customers like to see the people behind the organization, even if it is an e-commerce shop and nobody is actually seeing you. A friendly photograph goes a long way when it comes to building a relationship. This is the place for a personal touch.

Videos: Relevant and engaging videos will help keep visitors on your home page longer.

Since Google owns YouTube, you might want to use YouTube to host your videos. There is a good chance your video will rank higher on a Google search. Results are higher using YouTube than with other companies such as Vimeo.

Tip: Images play an important role for your online visibility. When you save an image to your computer, make sure the name attached to the image is one of your keywords, so when you upload the image to your website, it has that keyword saved in its title.

When people search for those keywords, they will see the images from your website in their search results pages. They will click on them, which will lead them to your website.

Links to sites with great free images:

http://kaboompics.com/

https://freerangestock.com/

http://www.everystockphoto.com

http://www.iconarchive.com/

Part 5: Social Media

Social media is a great way to promote and market your business alongside keyword implementation on your web pages.

There are numerous ways to utilize social media platforms to generate traffic to your site. What's important to remember is to focus your time and energy only on the platforms that your prospects are active on. It's pointless to post on Instagram or Twitter if your ideal customer doesn't use those platforms. To figure out which social media platforms are best for your business, go back to Part Two: Identifying Your Ideal Customer.

Here are my six favorite ways to utilize social media for my small business website:

1. Spread the word: Whenever I host a webinar or post a new article, I always have an option for those who registered to read or watch it to share a message about it with their friends and followers on Twitter and Facebook. This really helps expand the number of potential viewers for the webinar. Once someone registers and tweets or shares the message with his or her friends and followers, it creates a sense of a closed group that others would like to join (it's a good idea to reply to the people who took the time to post, and tweet to/message them with a personal welcoming message to deepen the relationship).

2. Share: Have this button handy under each blog post for easy sharing on Facebook, Twitter, Pinterest and Linked-In. My favorite plug-in is

Sharaholic; it is really easy to use, both for the readers and me.

3. Add a "Latest Post" box: This is one of my favorite options. By having the latest Facebook posts on my website's home page, I'm not only giving new visitors a way to follow and connect with me on Facebook, but it also shows them that the content is current and fresh. Also, the Face Pile widget allows for photos of friends to show up on your website who already liked your fan page. This widget is great for creating a sense of a closed community, as well as establishing the credibility of your site.

4. Connect with others in Google+ and Facebook groups: As a small business owner, you should know that it's not enough to have a promotion unless your current and prospective clients know about it, right? After a lot of experimenting, I found that Facebook and Google+ are the best platforms for spreading awareness for promotions. I simply joined the relevant groups and communities on those platforms where my ideal customers spend their time on. When I have a new promotion or article to share, I post it in those groups. (Note: Do not overdo on the sharing, or you might annoy and drive away potential clients).

Another very effective idea is to open your own groups on a topic that is related to your niche. This will automatically position yourself as an expert in your field. You can decide on the group's rules, host parties and challenges and promote your products. For example, my group on Facebook is

"Website Help for Serious Business Owners and Professionals."

5. Place a visible social media link on your website: What's the point of interacting via social media if your website's visitors don't see the links?

Just remember to set the links to your social media platforms so they open on a new page. This way, the social media page will not replace your website's page, and your prospects won't have to navigate away. Always make it easy for your clients to find your site without clicking the "previous page" button.

6. Lastly, and this is one of the best ways to leverage my social media channels and in order to send traffic back to my website and interact with my followers and prospects.

Send an automated "Thank You" email (with IFTTT) to each new Twitter follower with a free gift offer on your website. You can also automate a direct tweet to your new followers saying: "Thanks for following! Looking forward to your tweets. Here's a free gift that you will love: http://bit.ly/1SG2P39 "

If you don't have a freebie yet, you can just send your new followers to your latest promotion or to your website. However, it is most effective when you get them to sign up to your freebies as those new followers are hot leads. They followed you because they like what you have to offer or because they are searching for your services so you might as well give it to them.

The combination of a well built, professional website with the leverage of social media marketing and keyword implementation is very powerful.

Part 6: How to Reach More Clients Online

Now that you have a website with a solid home page and you understand the basics of social media, the next step is to generate traffic to your website. Here are three of the best ways to generate more traffic.

1. Blog

One of the best ways to generate traffic is through a blog.

Many business owners ask me if they should have a blog for their business, and my answer is almost always yes. A business blog can be utilized to help generate new clients in a variety of ways.

First, you can use the blog as a platform to share information with your prospects. The information could be about new services, new ideas, a checklist, a case study or a how-to article. If you are a fashion designer and summer is coming, create a series of blog posts about the latest styles and how to choose the best outfit for your body type. If you are a business coach, share some new publications on how to implement clever ideas in your business. This practice will help your prospects see that you are relevant and up-to-date.

Secondly, a blog can be optimized with keywords - terms and phrases which will help rank your website higher on Google and other search engine results pages. Take a moment to research those keywords. You can use tools like Google Analytics for free.

Google and other search engines' goals are to show their readers relevant and fresh content. Any new blog post will help them achieve that, and in return, will increase your chances of showing up on their first pages organically.

When readers comment on your blog posts, search engines regard those comments as an organic part of your blog post and if readers use some of your keywords in their comment that instantly gives your post another boost.

You can also use your blog to ask readers and followers to subscribe to your list.

Once your visitors and prospects sign up, start with "The Profit Funnel" process (see Home Page Must-Have 2). Send them two or three follow-up emails with even more information on the same topic.

In your fourth email, softly pitch your services by writing something like "Need my help with (the same topic you explored in the original post)? Let's schedule a call to see if I can help." Now they know you and how good you are. They most likely will call you, or at least remember you for the next time they experience the same problem.

Lastly, share snippets of your posts on social media platforms. This will send the traffic back to your website, and if your post is informative, rest assured that readers will browse the rest of your pages.

You may ask, "How often should I write and post on my blog?" It doesn't really matter; you can write and share once a day, once a week, once every two weeks or once a month as long as you are consistent and your content is relevant.

2. Smart social media marketing

From Facebook to Twitter, Snapchat, Periscope and Instagram, it seems a new platform pops up on the social media scene every day. However, there is no point in investing your time on every social media platform that is out there.

If your ideal customer is on Facebook, then you should also be on Facebook. If they are not using Twitter, Instagram or Pinterest, don't spend your time on those platforms.

You might be thinking, "I don't have the time for this, nor do I know what to share."

The good news is that there are tools and platforms like Hootsuite and Post Planner that allow you to pre-schedule posts weeks or months in advance. If you know your clients' interests and what benefits them, and you have 5 to 10 minutes a week, take advantage of these tools to pre-plan your posts so they include those interests and benefits.

3. Using webmaster tools such as Lexar, Bing Webmaster Tools and Google Analytics.

If you are serious about your online business, you should understand where your site's traffic is coming from; what keywords are people using to find you online? What pages do they enter on your site? From which page do they usually exit? How are your competitors doing? A webmaster tool will help gather all this information.

I see many business owners who are frustrated and confused. They have no clue if their prospects are resonating with their site's content or even how many visitors their site has every week.

If you know that your site's visitors are exiting from a certain page without taking any action, you might want to tweak your call-to-action in a way that will entice visitors to stay longer, or better yet, call you.

If you know that visitors are not spending any time on a specific page, you might want to check the content and see if it is relevant to your readers.

You can also figure out which websites are sending you the most traffic and strengthen your relationship with them.

This information is very valuable and it will help you take your business to the next level.

4. Keywords and optimization

The most basic and most important aspect of optimizing your website for Search Engine Optimization (SEO) is understanding keywords and what to do with them. So what are keywords? Keywords are the words that people enter on Google and other search engines in order to find something they are looking for. It can be one keyword or multiple keywords together, which is referred to as a "keyword phrase."

Your first step in this process is to figure out the specific keywords for your home page or any page on your site. Ask yourself, "What will my customers search in Google or Yahoo in order to find this particular page?" If it's your home page, ask yourself, "What are people going to look for to find my home page?" You might come up with more than one keyword or phrase for every page. How do you know which one to use? Use the one that will generate the most traffic; the one that most people are searching for.

There are many tools to measure this. Personally, I like to use Google Keyword Planner.

Where should you implement those keywords? In your pages' titles, URL, body and even images.

There are more advanced ways to do it, but that's for another book. My recommendation is to either spend some time researching this topic or find a professional who can assist you.

This can make a substantial impact on your site traffic.

Here are some websites that you can use to find your keywords:

Google Keyword Planner:

https://adwords.google.com/KeywordPlanner

Hootsute: https://hootsuite.com

PostPlanner : https://www.postplanner.com

Part 7: Common Website Mistakes and How to Avoid Them

Mistake #1 Choosing the wrong platform

Weebly, Wix or WordPress. Which platform should you use?

This is one of the most common questions I get from business owners, both beginners and established entrepreneurs. In fact, on every lecture I give or training I host, you can be sure this question will be asked.

Let me start by explaining the differences between the platforms.

Today, creating a website for an existing small business almost inevitably means choosing between a website builder and a CMS (Content Management System).

Both site builders and CMS's have pros and cons, and being able to identify these pros and cons is important in understanding which one will be better for your business.

Option 1:

Content Management System (CMS) is software that you or your web designer can install on your website that allows you to edit, tweak and publish content.

Pros:

1. These platforms are extremely flexible and can be customized and adapted to suit almost any business requirement.

2. CMS websites are free, but you still have to pay a monthly hosting charge or a domain charge to a third party (GoDaddy, BlueHost, etc.).

3. A site optimization feature is included in this platform and is very effective. Marketing your business online with this platform is fairly easy.

4. Once your website is up, it is easy to maintain the site. You don't need to hire an expert to update it for you.

Cons:

1. Most CMS platforms such as WordPress and Joomla are open source platforms. This means that their codes are open for everybody to use and modify. Any programmer/coder (and there are thousands of them) can use WordPress to create their own themes or plug-ins for others to download and use.

These tools could be fantastic or could be junk.

2. Updates and maintenance are extremely important, and you will need to do them regularly.

3. There is a learning curve with a CMS. There are so many themes, plugins and widgets to choose

from, that unless you are familiar with this platform, it can be a bit overwhelming and frustrating.

You might need to hire a web designer or a developer to put this site up for you.

Option 2:

Site builders (Wix, Weebly, school sites, Yahoo Site Builder, etc.).

Pros:

Website builders specialize in being able to provide highly custom web solutions without needing any technical skills. Web design involves a drag and drop interface that doesn't require coding.

Cons:

1. Usually, website builders charge a set monthly rate depending on your requirements. This cost includes the cost of hosting, upgrades and additional development.

2. Often, the site builder company's logo will appear in the bottom or header of your site and their URL will be part of your URL, which will make your business look unprofessional.

3. At the time of writing this book, SEO and marketing are not very effective with these types of platforms. Your visitors will have a hard time finding you online (unless they know your exact URL).

In summary, CMS websites almost inevitably have a fairly steep learning curve. However, once the site is up, you can easily take over and maintain it yourself, whereas site builder platforms are drag-and-drop, which means they are easier to use, and the process is faster.

However, when it comes to marketing and optimizing your website, site builder platforms are lacking in generating traffic and business to your site. When you build a website using one of the site builder platforms, you are basically getting a page under their website, so your site is a sub-site under their umbrella site. When you try to market and optimize your website, you are actually promoting the umbrella site and not your sub-site. This type of platform is for tiny businesses that have no experience or simply want as little hassle as possible. They don't yet think about generating business and new clients online.

As a business owner, the decision to use a CMS or a site builder depends on your business needs. Are you going to sell services and products online? Do you want to attract business and customers to your site? Or is your website just a placeholder and you don't need to attract new clients? Answer those questions, and you will know which platform is best.

Mistake #2 Not hiring a professional

The number one complaint I hear from new customers is, "Sarit, I hired someone to create a website for my business, but it's not what I really envisioned. It doesn't represent me, and when I contacted my web designer, he/she just disappeared; they never answered my calls/emails."

Your website is the online face of your business. You wouldn't hire a non-professional to plan your diet or even to paint your walls, so you shouldn't hire a non-expert to create your online presence. Your prospects will not do business with you if they don't like what they see online.

Before you decide on your web developer/designer, make sure they understand you and your vision. Make sure they will be there when you need them and that they are reliable.

Take the time to research them and their work. Read their testimonials, and take the time to call their previous clients.

Some web designers are also graphic designers, and some can even code. This is a huge benefit as they can design your logo and branding and keep everything aligned.

This will save you much time and money.

Lastly, make sure there is good energy between you and the web developer. Don't take this lightly. Creating a website is a very intimate and exciting process. You should feel good about those who work with you. Thankfully, there are many web developers and designers out there. Pick one you will enjoy working with and that understands your vision.

Mistake #3 The catch-22 syndrome

One of the other mistakes people make is waiting until they actually have a couple of clients before creating their website.

Business owners often say, "I don't have enough income right now. Maybe I should wait until I have a few clients before I invest in a website."

My question to them is: How is it going for you so far? Are you getting enough business online? Do people find you and hire your services? What is going to change?

While you hesitate, your competitors are establishing themselves online and getting all the business. Don't let it happen to you.

We all know that people are searching online now more than ever to find service-providers. Don't go to the movies or buy another coffee; use your savings or borrow the money. If you are serious about your online presence, and if you are motivated, do whatever it takes to invest in a good website, and start generating new clients and business.

How much should you reserve? What percentage of your income should you reserve for building a website or just maintaining it?

The answer is that there is no "one price fits all." Every business has its own requirements and needs.

A website with a shopping cart element and booking system will not cost the same as a website with a membership feature and a listing option.

The best way to figure this out is to sit down with your web designer and describe your business goals and vision.

This should help them come up with an accurate quote for you as well as the estimated time they need to accomplish the work.

Mistake #4 Replacing a website with a Facebook page

Do I really need a website? Can a Facebook page replace my website? The big issue with Facebook is that you own nothing. You might have followers or a large group of people that read your posts, but what happens tomorrow when Facebook decides to close that group? It has happened many times. You lose all of your followers' information: email addresses, names, telephone numbers, etc. Imagine if Facebook decides to block your account without warning; you have now lost all of your followers' names, friends of followers, comments, etc. You get the idea.

Every few weeks, Facebook posts new rules that members are required to follow: what you can post, what you can share, how many words you can put in ads, etc. Facebook may remove administrative rights or require you to change your page's name and Facebook web address for any page that fails to meet their requirements. Offers and advertising of your goods and services must, again, be subject to Facebook's advertising guidelines and page terms. Failure to comply with this policy will likely lead to your page being closed.

What if your ideal customer is not on Facebook? Facebook is a fantastic way to share information and generate traffic to your website, but it cannot replace a business website.

Furthermore, the number one issue that most people do not realize is that search engines like Google or Yahoo are not looking through Facebook posts, so your post on Facebook is only visible to your Facebook followers. That significantly reduces your internet exposure and marketing spectrum.

While Facebook can get you good interaction with followers, any particular post will not even reach 10 percent of your followers. Since Facebook wants to minimize your FREE exposure, it limits the number of followers who will see your posts. So you may have 1,000 followers, but only 100 – or even fewer – will see your posts.

Here are the benefits of having a website:

1) All search engines can find it!

2) You can optimize each and every page of your website with specific keywords.

3) You have an opportunity to present your business in the most positive and attractive light to potential new clients, without limitations.

4) You can manipulate the layout, fonts, pictures, and colors to reflect your style, business and services.

5) A blog on your website is a fantastic way to connect with your visitors; it's also a good way to keep your website current and fresh.

6) You can add, edit or remove pages and content when necessary.

What is the value of a Facebook page?

While it's clear that a Facebook page cannot replace a business's website, it is still a very important marketing tool if you know how to use it correctly.

A Facebook page is a very important soft marketing tool that offers interaction on a personal level. It does not offer the hard facts of who you are and how your business works. It's more laid-back, relaxed, fun and engaging. Facebook is a great tool to enhance and deepen your relationship with current clients and as such is a great complement to a website.

A great website can attract new customers, and along with a great Facebook page and strategy, can help you gain and maintain a loyal customer base.

Important links

Domain name and hosting:
http://www.bluehost.com (my preferred company)
http://www.godaddy.com
https://adwords.google.com/KeywordPlanner
http://www.wordstream.com/keyword-tool-google
http://www.leandomainsearch.com
Free images:
http://kaboompics.com/
https://freerangestock.com/
http://www.everystockphoto.com
http://www.iconarchive.com/

Keywords and insights:
https://adwords.google.com/KeywordPlanner
http://www.bing.com/toolbox/webmaster

Social media scheduling:
https://hootsuite.com
https://www.postplanner.com

One final thought:

I trust you've enjoyed reading this book and that you now have a better understanding of online business and what it really takes to create a successful website.

Growing your business is no longer just about building a beautiful website. In order to be SUCCESSFUL, your business must have the right strategy for growth, implemented in the right order, using the best-suited tools and systems while targeting the right type of customers.

My goal is very simple in this book: I want you to implement any of the tips I shared so you can see immediate results.

I also want you to focus your efforts and use your time and energy wisely and only where it makes sense for your business.

I tried to avoid jargon and fancy words and simplify everything for you, as I really believe that although you may not need all these tips, and should not do everything in your business, you still need to know what's involved so you can make the best choices.

How to Leverage Your Business and Generate New Clients Online

You already know your website is not generating the business you hoped it would. You've spent thousands of dollars and are wondering why no one is visiting it or buying from you.

You've experienced some traction in taking your business past the start-up phase but you know there's more you can do. The problem is getting out from under the day-to-day grind has been difficult. Sadly, you've become the bottleneck because you're still stuck working in your business, rather than strategizing and implementing new strategies for marketing and growth. What used to work is no longer working.

That's where we come in. We help business owners just like you leverage their business and generate new clients online.

Step 1: We will have an initial call to understand your vision and find out what your expectations and goals are for your online business and website. We will work with you to understand what isn't working and what will help to take your business to the next level.

Step 2: Based on our conversations and on your goals, we will brainstorm some layout strategies that will let your prospects know who you are and why they should be engaging with you. Our goal is to ensure that your site's visitors have every incentive to take the next step with you.

Step 3: We will implement everything we discussed and agreed on (your business goals, the best layout, marketing strategies and branding) into the designing and (re)building of your business website.

With us, you can leverage your talents into a highly engaging, targeted website that keeps working for you even when you are not.

We are happy to help. If you'd like to arrange a call, just visit **www.LotemDesign.com/contact** and sign up for a no-obligation strategy call.

www.ingramcontent.com/pod-product-compliance
Lightning Source LLC
Chambersburg PA
CBHW070359190526
45169CB00003B/1041